CONTRABAND COUNTY
SUSSEX SMUGGLING IN THE
19TH CENTURY

Forthcoming Title

Currently the author is researching material for another book. *Grave Smuggling Tales* will explore the history of smuggling through its tombstones. Many smugglers and revenue men lost their lives in the smuggling war which raged throughout the eighteenth and nineteenth centuries. Their epitaphs, supported by contemporary accounts from newspapers and customs records, tell the grim story of government's attempt to stem the flow of contraband and those who died in the struggle. The epitaph to Joseph Swaine (Figure 10) is one of many which will be gathered together in this book.

Contraband County
Sussex Smuggling in the 19th Century

Mark Bullen

Mark Bullen (signature)

Toby Press

Published by Toby Press
8 Mill Close, Blakedown, Kidderminster
Worcestershire DY10 3NQ

Printed by Severnside Printers Limited
Bridge House, Upton-upon-Severn
Worcestershire WR8 0HG

ISBN 1 898266 02 6

Contents

Figures

Acknowledgement: Figures 1, 2, 4, 5, 6, 7, 8, 9, 12 and 14 are reproduced by kind permission of Imperial Publishing Limited, sole licensees of the copyright holders Imperial Tobacco Limited.

Introduction

It is probably true to say that not many people have heard of the **Royal Naval Coast Blockade for the Prevention of Smuggling** (to give its full title). In view of its short life this is perhaps not surprising. It was born in 1817 and died a mere fourteen years later, to be replaced by the Coast Guard, the forerunner of our modern service.

The Coast Blockade was a Naval Force, administered by the Lords of the Admiralty. This story is not one about Customs Officers, Riding Officers or Revenue vessels, but about sailors, and landsmen (some specially 'imported' from Ireland for the task in hand). Notwithstanding this, the enemy was the same - the smuggler, at once the purveyor of contraband cargoes and the perpetrator of sometimes violent crime.

The aim of this short book is to cast a shaft of light onto this obscure body of men; to explain some of its failures and successes. If I have failed to convince the reader that the smugglers were not heroic figures, I hope at least that I have persuaded him or her that the Blockade men performed, for the most part, an honourable and arduous duty in the midst of bitter opposition from all sides.

'Smuggling, I am happy to say, is giving way on every part of the Line of Blockade ... and I am confident the Blockade will fully answer every expectation'.

Capt. W. McCulloch, October 1820

'The Blockade system is now in full operation in the county of Sussex; and, paradoxical though it may seem, so is smuggling also!'

Newspaper Correspondent, June 1830

A Sussex Landing

The night was black as pitch. The clouds, heavy and dark with snow, moved steadily across the winter sky. Viewed from the quiet bay the sea, too, looked threatening; powerful waves rolled in towards the shore, their white crests blown by the wind into salty spindrift. Crashing onto the beach, their furious energy spent, they dissolved in a creamy foam which seeped silently away between the rounded pebbles. The whole strand seethed with the continual shining movement of stones reclaimed by the strong Channel undertow.

The snow came, gently at first, then in more violent flurries, the soft white flakes falling sticky and wet, clinging to the driftwood and settling sparsely in the colder hollows of the high downland on either side of the estuary. What few trees there were stood desolate and cold. Bowed by the prevailing sou'westerlies, standing silent witnesses to the savage storms of the Sussex coast, they served to emphasise the loneliness of the spot. No friendly glow from a cosy parlour showed itself here, no moonlight lent enchantment to the rugged scene.

In the background, rising hundreds of feet sheer from the sea, stood a majestic line of white chalky cliffs, topped by the springy turf of the down. On this night the wind blew bitterly cold from the south-east, and several hundred yards from the beach, bobbing on the rough water, a smuggling lugger lay hove to, preparing to land her valuable cargo of foreign spirits. On a signal from this vessel the beach was at once a bustle of activity. Men, who five minutes earlier had been gathered in small groups in an effort to ward off the awful cold, were spurred into welcome action by the arrival of the first galley laden with tubs. Considerable strength and skill were required to bring this boat safely through the surf to discharge her goods and return for the next. As she beached, a number of men dressed in long coarse smocks were each loaded with a pair of small spirit tubs. Every man carried two half-anker

Figure 1: 'The Tub Man'. Half-anker tubs held 4½ gallons of spirit and were provided ready-slung for carrying.

barrels, joined by a cord harness slung across his shoulders. These 'tub men', most of whom were local labourers hired for the night, worked hard for their pay and made many trips from the sea to the waiting carts. Wooden planks were laid side by side up the shingle to stifle the sound of heavily laden carriers, and each horse wore special sacking over its hoofs. The oars of the long galley were likewise lagged as a precaution against splashing, while the men, if they had to, spoke only in hushed whispers. Now was the most dangerous and vulnerable time - the cargo only partly unshipped, the lugger trapped in the crescent of the bay, her crew busily engaged in supplying the rowing boat with another full load of kegs.

However, the smugglers were not without protection. To begin with, there were over a hundred of them. The majority of these were employed in the physical removal of the brandy. They were not armed and relied totally on the vigilance of the men engaged as watchers. In the event of surprise by any of the preventive forces a sufficient number of armed bullies stood by ready for action. These were the 'batmen', equipped with six-foot long ash poles, often iron-tipped and formidable weapons against anything but firearms. Many a preventive man's skull had been cracked with one of these sticks.

The batmen had split into two groups, one at either end of the beach and, during a quiet run of goods, were able to stand around smoking and gossiping. They had had strict instructions to keep away from the dangers of drinking, but none could resist keeping a secret hip flask under his shirt to combat the cold on bitter winter nights.

After half an hour, the run was nearly finished. All around, men began to relax, talking and joking now, anxiety giving way to relief. Suddenly, a loud shout rang out. 'Look out, lads, it's the preventives. Get the wagons away quick'.

A bright blue flare revealed the scene. A white, six-oared boat had crept unseen into the bay. One of the armed smugglers, a huge man, heavily bearded, cried in alarm, 'It's not the Customs, it's the Warriors again. Damn the Blockade, they'll not take us tonight'.

Figure 2: 'The Batman': 'armed bullies stood by ready for action'.

The organisers had worked well, for the goods were now being carried off towards Alfriston, some five miles inland. Provided the smugglers could keep the King's men occupied on the beach for a while all would yet be well. It wasn't the first time they'd been caught in the act of running a cargo, and it certainly wouldn't be the last. The Blockade galley stood some way off from the beach. At the stern was the man holding the blue flare; six more were rowing for all their worth towards the shore, while the others were attempting to fire at the remaining smugglers. This was not an easy task, for the boat bobbed and lurched violently in the heavy surf, and it was as much as they could manage for the revenue men to stay in their small craft. When they had beached and leapt ashore their problem immediately became apparent. Without the goods there could be no seizure; without horses or mounted reinforcements there could be no pursuit. Had they arrived even a few minutes earlier, when the carriers were heavily burdened with tubs, things might have turned out very differently. As it was, the smugglers were not obliged to strike a blow, even in self-defence. With the cargo safely away, and having caused a diversion at the other end of the beach to gain time, they mounted their horses and rode away into the darkness, leaving the Blockade men cold, wet and dispirited at the prospect of having to report another failure to their commanding officer.

The smugglers did not always get away. In August 1824, this very haven had been the scene of a more bloody encounter between them and a Coast Blockade party. Caught in the act of unloading a cargo of spirits, the smugglers had met fierce resistance.

'Whereas it has been represented to the Commissioners of His Majesty's Customs that between the hours of three and four o'clock in the morning of the first instant, William Williamson, a Quartermaster and Thomas Williams, a Seaman, belonging to His Majesty's ship *Ramillies* made seizure of a quantity of foreign spirits in Cuckmere Haven, in the parish of West-Dean in the County of Sussex, and that after they had made such seizure, they were violently assaulted by several Persons, who had collected upon the shore with a horse and cart for the purpose of conveying the said spirits away, and in his endeavours to secure two of the said Smugglers, the said William Williamson received five severe wounds upon his head and was otherwise much injured'.

In return for information leading to the arrest and conviction of the offenders, the Board of Customs offered the not inconsiderable sum of £50.

In those violent times there was scarcely a person who would speak against the smugglers, either from loyalty or fear of reprisal. Despite this, at the Winter Assizes the following December a certain Thomas Mills, 27, was charged with 'felonious and unlawful assembly, with others, to run smuggled goods', and also with the more serious offence of assault of a revenue officer.

Beginnings

The protracted and crippling war against Bonaparte finished in 1815. The navy had made a most valuable contribution towards his defeat; the war had provided shipbuilders with work and thousands of sailors with combat experience. In addition, it had kept the sailors from smuggling. In peacetime many of them had been fishermen or labourers. Some had volunteered for the service, while many others had been taken by the predatory Press Gangs which roamed every seaside town. Before the war such men had augmented their meagre wage by dabbling in a little 'harmless smuggling', either as boat crews, armed landsmen or tub carriers. Others, of more noble pedigree, had given considerable financial support to the venture. The war with Napoleon did not put an end to the trade - smugglers were welcomed enthusiastically by the French. Englishmen not only bought French brandy, lace and other dry goods, but connived in some cases in smuggling gold coin into France. Some were involved with espionage, providing the enemy with vital information about England's coastal defences and military disposition and strength. The smugglers had a field day: the Revenue Cruisers were at risk from privateers, the land preventive forces were vastly outnumbered, and the common people (almost without exception) supported the free-traders.

1815 brought dramatic changes. At a stroke the Admiralty had on its hands a large number of underemployed warships and sailors. Economy demanded that the majority of the fleet should be laid up, but the Admiralty were more anxious to dispose of the men in a way which would enable some of them to be recalled at short notice if need be. Paradoxically, while there were now more men available to combat smuggling, there were also many more who would return to their old peacetime habits as free-traders.

Parliament had been giving a great deal of thought to the ubiquitous smuggling problem. The 'heyday' of the trade had supposedly passed, but the Government was still losing vast sums of revenue through the illicit practices of smugglers all round the coast. Sussex and Kent, being nearest to the continent and the Capital, were most deeply involved. Stories of smugglers' effrontery, bravado and rough methods had spread to London; the public was fast losing confidence in the Government's ability to find a solution to the problem. England's morale, as well as her revenue, was at stake.

In 1816, *The Times* reported correspondence between the Treasury and the Revenue Boards of Customs and Excise concerning the better use of Revenue Cutters to prevent smuggling at sea.

In addition, a decision was taken to make more effective use of troops on the shore to supplement the work of the revenue vessels, by working in concert with them. At sea smugglers were often equipped with faster sailing craft and superior skills than the revenue crews. If circumstances warranted they could and did jettison their cargo in order to escape. It was one thing to lose a cargo, but quite another to lose the wherewithal for making a living - the vessel itself. Many smugglers who were caught were impressed into the navy for five years. Because smugglers were most vulnerable on land, and because a large number of tubs could be involved in one run, sizeable gangs of men were employed to spirit the contraband away from the shore to the multitude of secret stores in the hinterland.

The seaboard revenue officers were instructed by the Customs Commissioners to examine their particular stretch of coastline and advise

G. R. **IV.**

CUSTOM-HOUSE,
Newhaven.

Notice is hereby given, that there will be exposed for

PUBLIC SALE,

AT THIS OFFICE.

On TUESDAY, the 4th. of MARCH, 1823

AT TWELVE O'CLOCK AT NOON, IN SUNDRY LOTS;

THE BROKEN-UP HULLS

OF THE

FRISK CUTTER

AND A LARGE LUG-SAIL BOAT,

Together with the Anchors, Cables, Sails, and other Stores belonging thereto
Blankets, Counterpanes, Beds, and other Cabin Stores; and a small quantity of
Sheathing; also

A LARGE LUG-SAIL BOAT

With her Mast, Sail, and other Materials;

A SMALL BOAT; & SUNDRY BROKEN HALF ANKERS

*The Articles may be viewed on the day of Sale, and for further particulars apply to
Collector of Customs.*

H. HARISON.
J. B. STONE.

Custom House, Newhaven, February 13th. 1823.

Ruddock, Printer to His Majesty, Brighton.

Figure 3: Poster advertising a Sale of Confiscated Goods. It was one
thing to lose a cargo, quite another to lose the vessel itself.

on the most suitable places for stationing troops. Some idea of the expense which the Government was willing to incur can be gathered from the proposal to erect guard houses to accommodate them. The smugglers however knew the coast intimately and were able to land their goods more or less anywhere - whether on a flat shingle beach or under the cover of precipitous chalk cliffs.

The Customs Commissioners were directed 'to consider and to report, with the least possible delay, the extent of coast that should be allotted to the survey of each general surveyor, so as to afford the opportunity of a strict and constant vigilance of the conduct of the officers under him, and of the state of smuggling in his district'.

Despite the undoubted good intentions behind these ideas, Ministers failed to understand that there was an important obstacle to the employment of troops; the already bitter jealousy between the officers of the separate Customs and Excise services. Troops had been employed extensively in the previous century but were generally found to be disinclined to chase smugglers around the countryside, regarding it as degrading, unpleasant, and not a soldier's work. Last, but not least, they resented being given orders by civilians.

'Flogging Joey'

Captain William McCulloch R.N., a bright and able naval officer, found himself at the end of the war in command of *H.M.S. Ganymede*, stationed in the Downs for the prevention of smuggling. During 1816 he had been busily engaged in gathering intelligence about the activities of the Kent smugglers, and in July he wrote to Admiral Sir Charles Rowley, C-in-C Sheerness 'I have received information that a great number of boatbuilders have gone over to France from this part of the coast particularly Deal, Dover, Sandgate, Folkestone and Hastings for the purpose of constructing boats to run cargoes into this country'.

All of these towns, particularly the first and the last, were notorious for the smuggling activities of their inhabitants. Furthermore, not only were the French helping the English smugglers to build boats, but they were providing crews into the bargain. A correspondent to *The Times* reported that he had seen no less than eleven boats removing goods in broad daylight in the neighbourhood of Hastings, and 'they were all French vessels, whose crews, I am informed, are particularly expert in these fraudulent expeditions'.

At this time McCulloch was employing shore parties of sailors to good effect seeking out and destroying some of the many smugglers' hiding places. In this lay the germ of an idea. He had no doubt that the offshore patrols being carried out by the Water Guard were proving reasonably effective, but he fervently believed that the way to any real success was to hunt and hinder the smugglers on land at the same time. The Riding Officers of the Customs service were known to be almost useless against large bands of smugglers - indeed, when they were replaced some years later several were found to be octogenarians.

McCulloch proposed to use parties of hardy young sailors and did not underestimate the strength of the enemy. 'The smugglers here have been so long accustomed to carry every thing before them, by dint of terror and lawless fury, that they seem determined to try their effects either by intimidating or effectually removing me, the first they have failed in, and I really begin to think they mean if they can to shoot me in earnest. About ten days ago they fired at me on the Walmer Road, of which as well as other acts of abuse and violence I took no notice. I yesterday received a letter on board the ship informing me that a number of smugglers had determined to 'make away with' me and desiring me to be on my guard'.

Deal men had even been found prowling round McCulloch's home, to the great consternation of the Captain and his family. The local smugglers quite obviously saw in the proposed new system, and in McCulloch in particular, a serious threat to their livelihood. Murder, though quite beyond the pale, sometimes proved expedient. However, the Captain was faced with problems from within the preventive organisation as well as those posed by the smugglers.

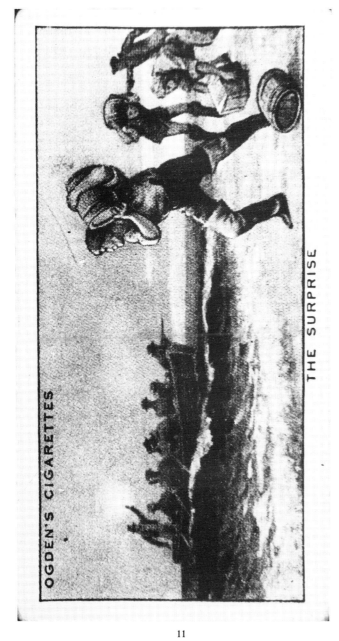

Figure 4: 'The Surprise': Rowing patrols were to be used in conjunction with shore-based men.

In February 1817 he wrote to Admiral Sir Charles Rowley at Sheerness 'Dear Sir, I am convinced that combining the two services in the Blockade of the coast, would be attended with the most important advantages. But I am afraid there will be some difficulty in blending the civil and military into the same service ... nothing can be more inefficient than the Preventive system as it now exists'.

Being of military mind, McCulloch believed that the problems he faced could be overcome by the application of disciplined men to the task. He thought that if the crews of the preventive boats and all the other forces engaged in the prevention of smuggling were subject to the same naval discipline, then he and they could not fail. Many of the preventive men on the coast were natives of the areas in which they were stationed - a situation hardly conducive to efficiency. Negligence and collusion were rife, the men profiting more by turning a blind eye than by doing their duty, with many being content to follow the line of least resistance.

McCulloch suggested a remedy - the boats should be manned by sailors and men should be posted away from their home territories. 'This would effectively crush the smuggling at once, and I am sure it would be mercy to the smugglers and their families. Should this arrangement not be convenient, I shall certainly do my utmost in watching over them continually, and keeping their attention to their duty. They have always been afraid of coming under my control and I am convinced they are as anxious to get clear of me as the smugglers are'.

McCulloch's faith in the power of strict discipline was firm, his trust in the efficacy of punishment no less resolute. It was not for nothing that he was later to earn the nickname of 'Flogging Joey' amongst the men of the Blockade.

The persuasiveness of McCulloch's ideas manifested itself in the Admiralty's agreement, in March 1817, to replace the Preventive Boatmen with sailors. Notwithstanding this, he was soon writing to the Admiral complaining of corruption amongst his own men. This was hardly surprising, for there was no reason to believe that sailors would be less willing to take bribes than Customs men. Fear of punishment was not a sufficient deterrent and reward money, if ever paid, was paltry compared with what the smugglers could offer. Reward money was divided between all the men regardless of effort or results, so that the lazy and inefficient men could profit from the exertions of others - clearly an undesirable state of affairs. The Captain thought that he could solve this by introducing a system which comprised reward according to results. Admiral Rowley replied that the smugglers would continue to raise the bribe in relation to the reward. He felt that McCulloch had placed too much faith in the honesty of his men, and suggested instead that the incentive of promotion should be coupled with 'a rigid observance of discipline', with recourse to courts martial when appropriate.

If he was unable for the time being to control all of his men, McCulloch did at least extract from his superiors the promise of a larger command vessel, the *Ganymede* being duly replaced in the Downs by the *Severn*.

The Blockade is Born

By a Treasury Minute of 19 June, 1817, the 'Coast Blockade for the Prevention of Smuggling' was officially established. *The Times* reported that the Government 'with a view to strengthen the measures already existing for the suppression of smuggling, have determined upon stationing a stated number of Lieutenants, 120 Midshipmen and 1,000 seamen on the coast of Kent and Sussex. It is intended that the officers and men should be divided into parties, each to occupy a Martello Tower. They are to keep watch by night, and thus, by their alacrity, intercept the acts of illicit traffic which the arrangements at present adopted are inadequate to prevent. They are to be victualled from the *Severn*'.

One reader, at least, was not impressed by this idea, referring to the men as a 'corps of Engineering douaniers', adding that 'a more weak, inefficient invention, I will undertake to predict, was never hit upon'. However, the correspondent was not entirely destructive in his forthright criticism - as an alternative strategy he proposed a halving of the duty on gin and brandy.

Initially, the Blockade was confined to the Kent coast between the North and South Forelands, but it was not long before its efficacy persuaded McCulloch to apply for an extension as far as Dungeness.

It was proposed that a number of galleys be provided for the Service, the men being quartered in block houses, other military posts, or in temporarily erected guard houses. Martellos provided the obvious answer, initially at least. The use of these buildings to house the new force could certainly not be attacked on the grounds of cost. These magnificent structures, modelled on a tower at Martello Point, Corsica, had been built at strategic spots along the southern and eastern coasts during the early years of the century as a defence against the expected French invasion. The walls, which could vary within the same tower from five to thirteen feet thick, were built of bricks set in a mixture of lime, ash and hot tallow (a concoction known as hot lime mortar) and were immensely strong. The roof was lead-lined and surmounted by a parapet six feet high and thick. A large cannon rotated on a central steel pivot. Several towers still survive, including one at Eastbourne used as a museum and a most unusual one, built to a quatrefoil design, at Aldeburgh. If nothing else, these towers were certainly capable of withstanding the attacks of even the most violent smugglers.

Blockade men, being sailors (though many landsmen were later employed), soon earned the nickname of 'men-of-war's men' or simply 'warriors'. They began to be a feature of the coastal scene, and when the Blockade was extended to Cuckmere Haven in 1818 many more citizens became familiar with the strange service. Public opinion about the Coast Blockade, not surprisingly, varied. Some thought it a splendid idea which was long overdue, while others considered it expensive and unnecessary. Many of its members were low quality naval ratings. A contemporary writer explained 'The roll [sic] is thus filled, for the most part - if by blue jackets, by 'waisters' [the least intelligent of a ship's crew] or, which is even more frequent, by unskilled though hardy Irish landsmen, whose estrangement from the sentiments, habits and religion of those placed under their surveillance seems to point them out as peculiarly adapted for

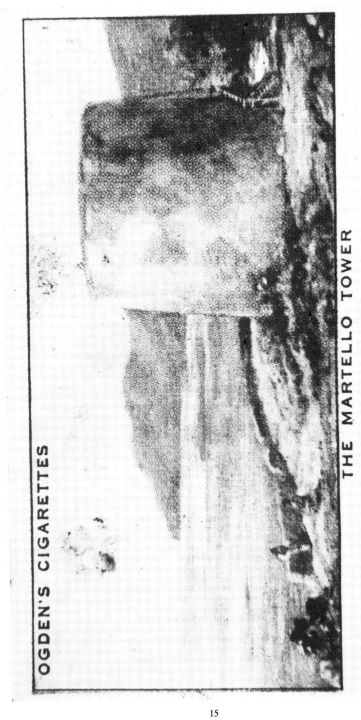

Figure 5: 'Martello Tower': Martellos were immensely strong and were situated at regular intervals along the Sussex coastline.

15

a service whose basis consists in a insidious watchfulness over others, and a hostile segregation from their fellow-men'.

The alien nature of the men seems to have been just what McCulloch thought he needed. It is true that many of the ordinary men in the Blockade were Irish - indeed, in later years ships were sent to Ireland on recruiting missions. There seems to have been no question of men being 'pressed' into the Blockade, from which they could (and often did) desert, and the Irish authorities were more than pleased to welcome the English ships, as is attested in the following letter sent from Cork. 'We the undersigned Magistrates of this neighbourhood beg you to accept our thanks for giving employment to so many of the poor inhabitants, which has and will be of future service to this part of the County as the redundant population were for a considerable time past in a state of starvation through the general want of employment; and we trust that should more men be required for the Service that you will be pleased to send your tenders to this or the Ports adjacent when those wanted will be speedily furnished'.

The smugglers in the southern counties of England had become so used to having their own way, by means of a bribe here and there and the occasional 'misunderstanding' with an overzealous official, that the Blockade came as something of a shock to them. In October of 1817 McCulloch, surprised perhaps, but not deterred, wrote 'the smugglers do not by any means stand in fear of the force we can oppose to them, being only deterred from violence by the dread of legal penalties ... I have received information from the most respectable persons in this neighbourhood that the smugglers are determined to resist the system of Blockade'.

During the late eighteenth century, Sussex smugglers had proved themselves to be a particularly vicious strain, quite different from their generally more gentle West Country cousins. A reward advertisement from a local newspaper of 1819 indicates the sort of treatment a Blockade man could expect. John Aston, stationed at Pevensey Sluice, was attacked by the crew of a lugger, the *Fox* of Bexhill, 'who knocked down the said John Aston, walked over him, and bruised, and ill-treated him', the weapons used being bludgeons and stones.

Figure 6: 'The Warrior': Blockade men were known as 'Man-of-War's Men' or simply 'Warriors'.

The following year McCulloch reported 'the smugglers lately attacked the line of the Coast Blockade in great force, and although they have been repulsed in the most spirited manner by our parties ... we are at present rather weak in numbers'.

It is interesting to note here the comment that the force was considered to be understrength, there being between Cuckmere Haven and Camber (a distance of some 35 miles or so) no fewer than 30 Blockade stations. These ranged from the sparsely manned Haddocks Watch House near Hastings, with seven men, to Hastings itself with thirty-eight, and the guard-ship *Enchantress* based in Rye Harbour with a complement of twenty-five. In addition to the Lieutenants, Midshipmen and Admiralty Mates there were 363 men based along this stretch of coastline. This may seem rather a lot, but one must bear in mind the frequently large bands of smugglers, the Blockade's difficulty in securing sufficient reinforcements in case of sudden need, and the great expanse of countryside to be patrolled. When intelligence of a run was obtained, the men from the different parties invariably joined forces, a greater chance of success consequently being enjoyed. With regard to the problems of effective and prompt communication between patrolling parties, it must have been gratifying to see in December 1820 the completion of a semaphore system linking stations between Beachy Head and Deal. A request was immediately made for the men to be issued with signal books and spying glasses.

McCulloch's mood seems to have changed rapidly, for only a few days after the last pessimistic report he was commenting 'Smuggling, I am happy to say, is giving way on every part of the Line of Blockade ... and I am confident the Blockade will fully answer every expectation'.

Organisation

In 1820 a survey of the Kent and Sussex coasts was undertaken by one of the Lords of the Admiralty, accompanied by Sir John Gore, Port Admiral of Sheerness. Their opinion of the new system was not flattering, mostly on account of its expense. Notwithstanding their criticisms however, when major changes were introduced in the following year to the organisation of the whole of the preventive force, the Coast Blockade was left untouched, Government believing that it had proved itself sufficiently effective.

The Coast Blockade along the Sussex coast was divided into three administrative Divisions, each of these being sub-divided into four districts. The Eastern Division of the Sussex Blockade extended from Camber watch house to Langley Fort near Eastbourne, while the Central Division ran from Tower No. 71, Eastbourne to Shoreham. When the Blockade was eventually extended along the whole length of the Sussex coast, the Western Division stretched from Shoreham to the boundary with Hampshire.

Each district was under the command of a junior Lieutenant, and consisted of a party of about ten men, each of which had roughly a mile of coastline to patrol. Not a great distance, one might say, but imagine the conditions in which the men often had to work. They were divided into two watches, causing them to be out six hours each during the night. Much of their patrol beat comprised wild and dangerous countryside, with stretches of high vertical cliffs. Revenue men, (no matter to which service they belonged), and all that they represented, were almost universally hated. On dark stormy nights the dangers were sufficient without the constant threat of abuse or physical violence. Clifftop 'accidents' were not infrequent, and one can only surmise whether the terrain and the weather were alone responsible for the many falls.

A Blockade man, named Sullivan, was killed by falling from the cliff top near Beachy Head. A correspondent to a local newspaper was not happy. 'This is not, by a great number, the first death that has occurred in the same way. It is surely a wanton exposure of the lives of these poor men, to compel them to walk the hills on such nights as that. It was utterly impossible for a smuggler to have landed that night, and it must therefore have been quite unnecessary to have sent out the men to parade to and fro upon the downs, at the very edge of the cliff, where to save themselves from the danger of falling over, even on ordinary nights, they are obliged to trust to the guidance of large chalk stones, which are

OGDEN'S CIGARETTES

THE MIDSHIPMAN

Figure 7: 'The Midshipman': Each patrol was lead by a Lieutenant or Midshipman.

laid thickly along upon the dark turf, from one point of their station to the other. On the night in question the accident most probably happened from the snow, which prevented the poor fellow from seeing the chalk that was intended to be his guide'.

It seems most likely that the charitable writer was correct to infer that the weather was the direct cause of the tragedy, though it cannot always have been the case. However, he grossly underestimated the smugglers' determination, for a report two days earlier had stated that on a night when, 'owing to the drift of the snow, the Blockade men on duty were unable to see more than a few yards before them', smugglers landed 300-400 tubs at Elmer, near Littlehampton.

Many other men were hurt or killed around the cliffs. In April 1824 Mr. Michell, a Midshipman, walked over the cliff near the Wish Tower, Eastbourne, sustaining a fractured arm and bruises, from which he fortunately recovered. The following month another went over, this time with fatal consequences, the accident being caused by fog. Thomas Wadham disappeared over the edge, it being supposed that he had dozed off while on patrol. This is not as unlikely as it seems, for the men must have been at times desperately tired. In later years they were issued with one-legged 'donkey stools' which prevented them from falling asleep whilst on duty (or at least, woke them up if they did).

Another Blockade man, William Harford, stationed at Saltdean Gap, fell over a 90 foot cliff near Porto Bello Gap, fracturing his skull. In the course of the enquiry it was revealed that he had been in the habit of approaching the cliff edge and peering over it; he paid dearly for his attention to duty. Perhaps the most bizarre example of such an accident concerned a certain John Brand, who managed to end his own life while **climbing** the cliffs at Holywell. At first it was thought that he was drunk, as he had just been paid, but enquiry revealed that it had been his hobby to scale the chalk cliffs for pleasure.

Apart from falls and attacks by smugglers, more curious misfortunes befell the men. Whilst engaged in pistol target practice near Beachy Head, one Blockade man accidentally shot a comrade through the thigh, while at Newhaven a sailor was painting the sides of the guard

Figure 8: 'The Shears': The Blockade man fell into the smugglers' basket and was winched to the top of the cliff.

vessel when his tackle gave way and he was thrown into the water, whereupon he sank, luckily only temporarily.

The men stationed along the parts of the Sussex coast which were protected by cliffs had the additional problem of having to patrol both the beach and the cliff top. They patrolled the foreshore until the rising tide made it imperative for them to ascend the cliffs. This often involved a lengthy and time-consuming walk, and it was then that the Blockade was vulnerable to a run of goods. A common and clever smugglers' ploy was the use of a portable derrick which was assembled on the cliff top, a rope and basket then being lowered to the shore via a well-greased pulley. Tubs or other goods were thus hoisted up the face of the cliff without danger of discovery. On one remarkable occasion the smugglers were somewhat premature in setting up their apparatus. A Blockade man was hurrying along the shore, perhaps to escape the rising tide, when he bumped into the basket which had been lowered. He fell in and was promptly jerked to the top in the belief that he was the first load of contraband. On arrival he had the presence of mind to sound the alarm by firing his pistol, at which point the smugglers, not surprisingly, scattered, leaving their adversary with the goods.

Another rather amusing incident concerning the use of a derrick occurred in August, 1821, when an attempt was made at Rottingdean to haul a number of tubs up the cliff in the manner described. However, the smugglers had not succeeded in getting up more than five or six casks before a flint fell from the cliff and struck one of them on the head. On this the wounded man ran screaming into the sea, and a Blockade galley pulled into the shore, resulting in the seizure of the smuggling boat complete with a cargo of about fifty tubs.

On other occasions the small barrels were covered with plaster of Paris, to imitate lumps of chalk, left on the open beach and collected later with a horse and cart. More enterprising smugglers spent nearly two weeks cutting out a shelf in the chalk cliff two hundred feet above the beach. It was not uncommon in those days for shepherds to go down the cliffs hunting for birds' eggs, so the work was carried out under the very noses of the Blockade patrols. The excavated ledge was invisible both

OGDEN'S CIGARETTES

THE FIGHT

Figure 9: 'The Fight': The men went about their work in a rough, bull-dog sort of fashion.

from above and below and proved invaluable as a totally safe intermediary storage area.

Blockade sailors were well-armed, carrying a cutlass and a brace of pistols; at night they also added a musket and bayonet. In these early days there was no separate 'preventive' uniform, so the Blockade wore clothing in the naval style of the day, adapted for their own use: 'worsted stockings, stout shoes that cover above the ankles, flannel drawers, thick blue trousers made on purpose and supplied gratuitously to the men, flannel waistcoat next the skin, over their shirts a stout woollen Guernsey jacket, a common blue jacket and over that supplied as the trousers are a stout blue pea jacket reaching below the knees and worsted gloves'.

Many of the men wore extra clothing during spells of very cold weather, but any man who still suffered badly was supposed to be removed to the watch house until he recovered. In the summer the men wore straw hats with white trousers and frocks. Higher ranks wore the naval uniform and were less heavily armed, usually relying on a sword alone for protection. Blue flares were carried by all patrols and were frequently used to summon assistance.

The carrying of weapons was necessary, given the circumstances and the risks involved. It did, on many occasions, save the lives of the Blockade men, but it must also have been an encouragement to the smugglers to equip themselves similarly. The arming of the force did nothing to improve its image with the local population, as is attested by the comment that the men 'went about their work in a rough, bull-dog sort of fashion. They went out heavily armed, and were not slow in using their arms. I have been informed by credible persons that if they wanted to enter a house in which they suspected any smuggler was concealed, they would unceremoniously smash open the door with the butt-ends of their muskets, and when inside would bundle women and children, bed and all, on to the floor'.

In view of the brutality of many smugglers, one can hardly be surprised that the men of the Blockade sometimes conducted their 'enquiries' with a certain lack of finesse and chivalry.

The Swaine Affair

1821 was a crucial year for the Blockade. Several incidents, and one in particular, brought to the forefront of public opinion the question of the force's powers of search. Up to this time, the men of the Blockade had been employed to seek out and seize physically, where possible, smugglers. However, what was becoming more and more clear to McCulloch and the smugglers was that the presence of relatively large numbers of Blockade parties made smuggling more difficult. Smugglers began to resort to cunning and guile to achieve their purposes. To keep pace with this development the Blockade needed powers to search vessels, in particular fishing boats. It was the desire to search such a boat which lead to a tragic death and a public furore which the Blockade was fortunate to survive.

Hastings had long been a notorious haunt of smugglers. The old town community which had been dependent on fishing and smuggling bitterly resented the presence, and the manner, of the armed seamen perpetually hindering them in their honest, and not so honest ways.

First, a word or two of explanation is needed about the method of berthing fishing boats at Hastings. Then, as now, it was the practice to winch boats up the shingle beach to above high water mark. In March Captain McCulloch received a letter of complaint from the Mayor of Hastings regarding the Blockade's rummaging methods. The men had been in the habit of rummaging fishing vessels **after** they had been winched out of the water but **before** they were berthed, a system which caused great inconvenience to the fishermen. The reasons for the procedure adopted were first, that to have searched the vessel whilst still in the sea would have entailed the Blockade sailors wading up to their waists in water - a duty guaranteed to discourage all but the most diligent of them - and secondly, that to have searched them after they had been berthed would have subjected the men to constant jostling from the hostile crowds. Furthermore, the market would provide the ideal place to dispose of any contraband before the rummage could take place. The fact was that neither practice was conducive to an efficient search - McCulloch's primary concern, and he summarised his feelings to the

Mayor thus: 'It appears to me that their being prevented from doing (perhaps a little) business in illicit trade, is the only cause of their discontent'.

Fair comment, no doubt, but it must be stated that boats being rummaged in the disputed fashion were liable to topple over from their unsupported position if boarded by an overzealous official.

On the morning of Tuesday 13th. March, George England, a Blockade seaman stationed in the town, was patrolling the beach. As he did so, Joseph Swaine, a local fisherman, was winching his boat up the shingle. England requested to search the vessel, at which Swaine resisted, explaining that he would be quite willing for the search to be carried out as soon as he had manoeuvred his boat into a more suitable and stable position. 'This promise, however, did not suit the Blockade man, he immediately got into the boat, and was followed by Swaine, when a sort of scuffle ensued ... soon after which, in an angry altercation, the Sailor drew a pistol, and, horrid to relate, shot Swaine through the body'.

Despite protestations that it was an accident, England was arrested and tried for murder. From the evidence related at the trial, which caused much public interest, it appears that the death arose as a direct result of two factors: first, as already discussed, the method of search employed, and secondly, the fact that the Blockade carried firearms. The prosecution furnished nine witnesses, comprising labourers, fishermen and mariners. Their version of the story was that Swaine had been working his boat up the beach aided by his partner, William Tassel. The former had been at the windlass while the latter was holding the boat upright until it was properly berthed. It was Tassel who addressed England first, explaining that if he (England) were to board the vessel, she would topple over. England had ignored his plea and climbed in to commence his rummage. On realising this to be the case, Swaine, no doubt incensed by what he regarded as an unreasonable attitude, leapt aboard and became involved in a scuffle. The two wrestling men fell out onto the beach, whereupon England drew his cutlass and attempted to strike Swaine, who was unarmed. Having his sword knocked from his hand and into the sea, England drew his pistol and another struggle

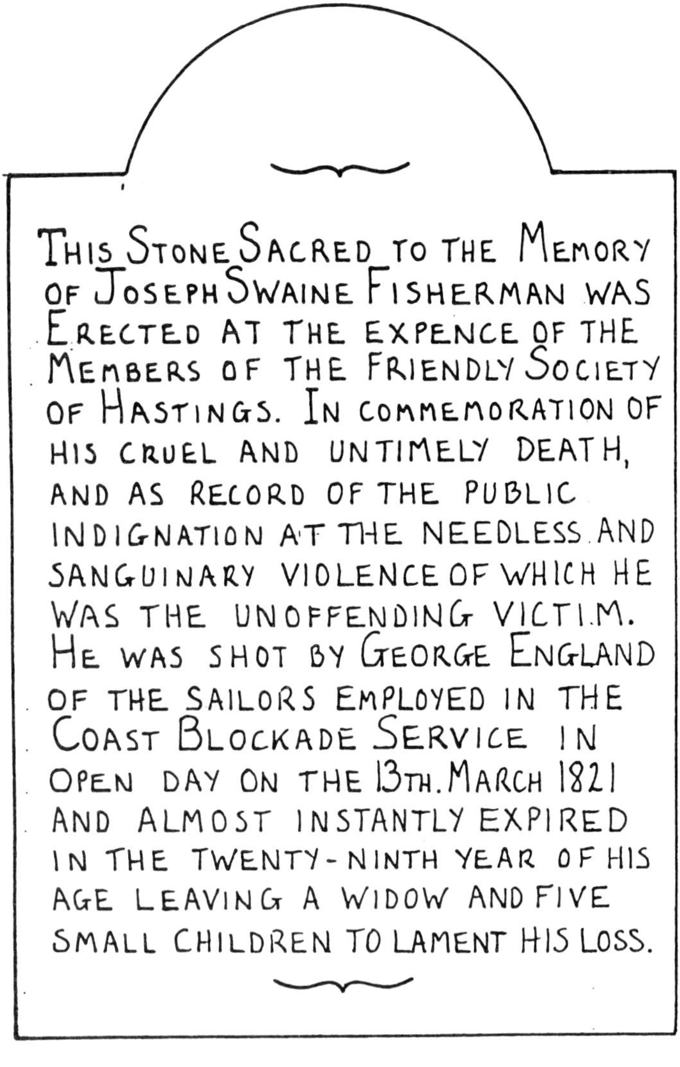

THIS STONE SACRED TO THE MEMORY
OF JOSEPH SWAINE FISHERMAN WAS
ERECTED AT THE EXPENCE OF THE
MEMBERS OF THE FRIENDLY SOCIETY
OF HASTINGS. IN COMMEMORATION OF
HIS CRUEL AND UNTIMELY DEATH,
AND AS RECORD OF THE PUBLIC
INDIGNATION AT THE NEEDLESS AND
SANGUINARY VIOLENCE OF WHICH HE
WAS THE UNOFFENDING VICTIM.
HE WAS SHOT BY GEORGE ENGLAND
OF THE SAILORS EMPLOYED IN THE
COAST BLOCKADE SERVICE IN
OPEN DAY ON THE 13TH. MARCH 1821
AND ALMOST INSTANTLY EXPIRED
IN THE TWENTY-NINTH YEAR OF HIS
AGE LEAVING A WIDOW AND FIVE
SMALL CHILDREN TO LAMENT HIS LOSS.

Figure 10: Epitaph to Joseph Swaine, formerly in All Saints churchyard, Hastings

followed. Meanwhile, several more men from *H.M.S. Severn* arrived and succeeded in grabbing hold of the fisherman, who promised to go with them as a prisoner to the watch house. It is here that the evidence of the two sides is at variance. The prosecution contended that England had aimed at Swaine and shot him in cold blood, while the defence maintained that the pistol had discharged accidentally in the scuffle. We will never know the truth.

George England was found guilty at the Horsham Assizes, but to the utter horror and disbelief of the Hastings fishermen, the death sentence was not passed. A writer to the *Sussex Weekly Advertiser* summed up the point of law. 'The witnesses for the prosecution say, that **aim** was taken, but those for the defence deny it. As to the question of **murder**, this difference is immaterial - For if a man, **who is armed**, in the discharge of his duty is resisted, and a scuffle ensues, and heat of blood is engendered, and if the armed man kill the other, before there is time for the parties to cool, it is only Manslaughter in him, under any circumstances, although it is in almost every possible case, **murder** in the other'.

The writer concluded on a salutary note. 'It is to be hoped that this lamentable case, on the one hand may lead to some well considered regulations respecting the exercise of this very obnoxious duty of search; and on the other, may teach those who are subject to it, the necessity of submitting to it peaceably, and when they have any complaints that are grounded, to apply for legal redress'.

Politically, of course, the tragedy had immense implications, highlighting as it did the acrimonious and continual running battle between the revenue forces and the coastal populace. Parliament was not long in debating the issue. Mr Curteis, a Sussex MP, laid before the Commons a notice that a return should be made of 'all inquests which have been taken on the bodies of all persons who have lost their lives since the institution of the Coast Blockade and Preventive Boat system, by reason of any circumstance arising from or connected with smuggling, or the protection of the Public Revenue'. It was also proposed to ask Commanding Officers of the Blockade for a list of men wounded or killed in the course of their duty. Curteis maintained that a system which led to such violence and loss of life must be radically bad, and that the price being paid for the eradication of smuggling was too high. Twenty-five people had been killed and numerous others mutilated and maimed for life in the skirmishes. He contended that while such temptingly high duties existed then so too would smuggling on a vast scale, imploring Ministers to lessen these duties in favour of other forms of taxation, if only for the sake of humanity. McCulloch referred to the increasing violence of the smugglers, stating pessimistically, 'Whenever they determine to disregard the laws, and cease to dread the Verdict of a Jury, we have no force to withstand them'. In many cases of course, the smugglers were right not to dread any verdict, pronounced as it often was by a jury comprising entirely local, and thus sympathetic, persons. For this reason more important trials were held in London, where evidence could be examined in a more just and dispassionate way.

In due course another MP called for a revision of the Revenue Laws. According to him, 'The alarm is now such that all the fishermen at Hastings have drawn up their boats, and the whole population is in terror of the recurrence of these dreadful atrocities'. He stated furthermore that **dozens** of people had been put to death along the South Coast, and that the murders should not be allowed to continue, 'to prevent gin or lace from being now and then landed'. The Chancellor of the Exchequer for one was not in total sympathy with this opinion. He believed first, that the judge was correct to show George England mercy and secondly, that most of those living on the coast were engaged in smuggling and that their disposition could only be repressed by 'moderate yet efficacious measures'. Another member was anxious to know whether the government intended to change the system under which it was actually dangerous to live on the coast. The reply came that the officers and men engaged in preventive work had behaved with the utmost moderation. The government had tried to dispense with searching fishing boats but results had proved it necessary to continue doing so. Such regulations as existed attempted to make the duty of search as unburdensome as possible, but little would satisfy the people except the liberty to smuggle.

Searches and Seizures

During the course of the next few years the authority to search fishing vessels thoroughly was to become an extremely important weapon in the armoury of the preventive forces. In March of 1822 a report came from Rye that several clever concealments were being found in such boats as a result of rummage operations. Hollow keels were found with tin pipes inside containing tubs of spirits. Every possible place where goods could be hidden was employed in an effort to outwit the authorities, and many concealments were specially constructed as the preventive men gained intelligence. At Rye a Blockade man had seized a punt which was in effect a **double boat**, there being a gap of three inches between the inner and outer planking which contained 400 pieces of French cambric, covered with silk oilskin. In November 1824 a fishing smack, the *Diamond* of Rye, a cutter-rigged, 25 ton vessel, was seized by Lieutenant Dicken of the Coast Blockade stationed in the town. In the course of the rummage, concealments were found under the ballast and 33 various sized tubs of foreign spirits were revealed (see Figure 11).

The officer's report stated 'I bored with a gimlet through the bulkhead which secures the ballast forward and bored into something which I clearly felt was not shingle. I therefore commenced removing her ballast which consisted of first shingle, next two tins of iron closely stowed, and under which another layer of shingle. On removing this I discovered a platform under which were four trunks of sufficient breadth to contain one tub each and about twelve feet long. The trunks are loaded by entering the tubs at the foremost end and pushing them aft, a line being fastened to the aftermost tub to draw them out again. To prevent detection from **boring** each trunk was footed at its foremost extremity next the bulkhead with a small box the shape of the trunk and about three inches wide, one inside of which was lined with iron. This box was filled with shingle so that **in boring** your gimlet would penetrate the box and get into the shingle and passing through it come against the iron plate which would lead you to suppose you were touching the iron ballast'.

The Blockade's powers of search constituted a thorny problem. In July 1822 a fracas was reported at Hastings (again) when the Blockade detained a basket of fish in order to rummage it. Nor was it only ordinary

The *Diamond* of Rye

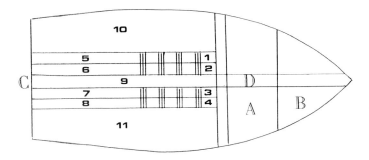

1-8   Boxes made to fit into the trunks and so placed as to be easily lifted out to remove the tubs. These boxes are filled with shingle so that you may bore into them through the bulkhead **A**, their after side cased with iron.

B   The forepeak.

C   The cabin bulkheads.

D   The keelson.

9   "   "

10,11   The wing ballast.

A strong platform of inch wood covered the trunks and came close forward to the bulkhead **A**. On this platform the ballast was stored which was covered by a platform strongly battened down.

Figure 11: Diagram of the concealment found by Lieutenant Dicken on board the fishing smack *Diamond*.

folk who were subjected to the Blockade's attentions. The month after the fishy incident no less a person than the Duke of Norfolk was involved in a rummage. On this occasion he and others had been on a yacht excursion from Eastbourne to Hastings. On their return a bundle of silk stock was detained for examination, but was released on the orders of the commanding officer on his being given a plausible explanation as to the silk's origin. A week later another important personage was the victim of a search. Lord George Bentinck had arrived at Eastbourne from Hastings and, 'he then had to undergo the unpleasant ordeal of having his personal luggage stopped by the Coast Blockade men (who very properly execute their orders). A Customs Officer arrived to convey it to the Custom House, some ½ mile away. After a message being sent, the Collector himself arrived to clear the luggage'.

The legal right of the Blockade to carry out such searches was thrown into some doubt by a newspaper article appearing in June 1824. Here, reference was made to the 'want of authority to search, which appears to have been inadvertently omitted in the Act (57 Geo Chap 7 Sec 20)', under which Blockade men held a deputation from the Board of Customs. However, this fact seems to have had little effect on their zealous execution of their duty.

In September 1825 the *Sussex Weekly Advertiser* warned 'Travellers in the silk and ribband trade should be cautious how they proceed by sea with their goods, in pursuing their journeys from place to place, as two gentlemen lately left Brighton in luggers for Hastings, but in consequence of the wind becoming shy, they were obliged to land at Seaford, and by having merchandise unaccompanied by any official documents, the whole was on being landed seized by Lieutenant Clayton, R.N. belonging to the Coast Blockade, and conveyed to the Custom House, Newhaven'.

Some of the goods were restored immediately but others, appearing to be of foreign manufacture (because of their high quality), were sent to London for examination, notwithstanding the apparently respectable demeanour of the owners. The newspaper concluded 'In the above seizure there is novelty, and it will probably induce these traders, in future, to make their coasting trips by land than by water; and especially

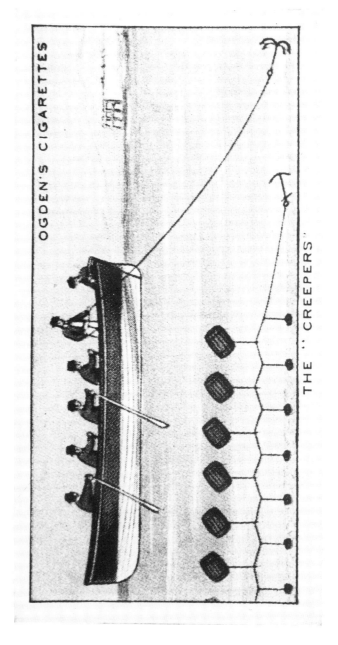

Figure 12: The Creepers': Searching the sea bed for barrels with a 'creeping iron'.

as a week's detention may be of some consequence to the sale of such fancy articles'.

With the introduction of a cross-channel packet service in the 1820s the temptation to secrete such 'fancy articles' about her person persuaded many an otherwise law-abiding lady to dabble in contraband.

Another item of suspect origin was a six-quart tub of spirits found floating in the sea at Eastbourne by John Hide, a local fisherman. Whilst in the act of making off with his find he had the misfortune to run into two Blockade men who bade him stop and surrender the cask. Panicking somewhat, he dropped it, whereupon the staves broke and the contents were lost. He was taken into custody for being in possession of smuggled goods, found guilty and sentenced to five years naval service. The reporter of this incident was aghast at the fate of the poor fisherman. 'Some distinction should be made between a man going to the seaside for the express purpose of assisting to run goods, and another who accidentally picks up a cask of spirits from the sea, and endeavours to secure it as his lawful prize'. This case was a clear indication of how harsh the law could be in circumstances which quite obviously required a degree of moderation to be shown. A petition was sent to London pleading the man's good character and innocence of any criminal intent.

The craftiness of the smugglers was increasing weekly, and some methods of concealment were remarkably ingenious. During the early 1820s there was an aeronaut called Green who had been drawing crowds wherever he appeared with his air balloon. In December one year he was active around Seaford and was frequently seen flying over the Seven Sisters cliffs. During a gale, inhabitants of nearby East Dean saw what they thought to be Green's airship, and several humorous theories were proposed to explain the phenomenon. A former Riding Officer suggested that it was a contrivance adopted by the smugglers to elude the vigilance of the revenue officers by carrying contraband goods by clockwork. Meanwhile, the object of their conjectures had stuck fast in a clump of furze bush. Armed with flails and pitchforks, they approached to investigate it closer and, to the astonishment of all present, found it to be a long galley, painted white, belonging to the Coast Blockade stationed at Birling Gap. The violence of the wind had lifted the boat into the air and blown it across the hills to a spot at least a quarter of a mile from where it had previously been.

Extension

'The report lately propagated, that the coast blockade service was about to be broken up, is entirely unfounded; on the contrary it is understood to be in the contemplation of Ministers to extend the limiting of that service to Portsmouth and Orford Nap ... even its most violent opponents admit that it has annihilated smuggling within the limits of its jurisdiction ... let but his Majesty's Ministers establish the law which we have advocated, and extend the boundaries of the aforementioned officer's [McCulloch's] system, and it needs no prophet's skill to predict that illicit traffic must inevitably disappear, and the revenue of the customs continue to increase'.

There is no question of smuggling having been annihilated but there **was** evidence to suggest that the Blockade was having a significant effect - smugglers began to move their operations westward as the Blockade increased its grip in the east. In the spring of 1822 several watch houses were constructed in the Eastbourne area for the sole use of the Coast Blockade - 'their general convenience and neatness reflects credit on the projectors, and the excellent arrangements are highly creditable to the skill of the commanding officer, Lieut. Chappell'.

Chappell was without doubt a most diligent officer and felt proud of the men under his command and of the job they were doing. Hence his sensitivity to newspaper articles appearing in November 1821 implying that the smugglers were enjoying great success in the eastern part of the county, whilst in the west they were sustaining great losses. Chappell wrote in defence to the *Brighton Gazette*, saying that such rumours were often put about by Custom House and Riding Officers, jealous of the Blockade successes.

'Having thus asserted my ability to prove that the smugglers residing here (Eastbourne) go for safety to run their cargoes in the

western part of this county ... **there are necessarily most seizures made, where most smuggling is carried on**'.

Against this last statement there was of course no argument, it being impossible to prove or disprove. Notwithstanding Chappell's loyalty to his own men, there appears to have been a great deal of truth in his statement that much smuggling was being carried out to the west of the Blockade limits. There were numerous reports that goods were being landed in West Sussex, thence to be conveyed by cart back to Eastbourne, Hastings or even Rye. A writer to the *Brighton Gazette* advised that smugglers 'frequently travel on foot thirty or forty miles in a night ... scarcely a single dark night passes but smuggled goods are landed to the **westward** of Cuckmere Haven, whereby the whole **western** part of the county is inundated with contraband commodities'. According to the correspondent, in Brighton smuggled gin was plentiful, together with gloves, silks and laces 'it is a matter of surprise to most persons, that government should suppress illicit trade with such extreme rigour **east** of Beachy Head, while every facility is afforded for our Sussex smugglers to carry on their speculations in the **west**'. Perhaps the ultimate proof of these contentions came in a letter to Captain McCulloch suggesting that an Eastbourne smuggler named George Harrington had been 'playing the very devil in the Isle of Wight and Southampton'. This entrepreneur had run his goods at Lymington and brought them back eastwards inland.

In the face of such evidence, the government gave its blessing to the extension of the Coast Blockade westwards, covering the whole of the Sussex coast and beyond.

Lives Saved and Lost

The lifeboat service was not introduced until 1824. During its early years, and those immediately preceding its birth, the men of the Coast Blockade performed a very useful function in helping to save the lives of shipwrecked sailors. In spite of all the ill-feeling caused by the death of Joseph Swaine at Hastings, the local paper had the good grace and honesty to report that 'The establishment of the Coast Blockade is an object of the greatest importance, as far as it affects merely the mercantile interests of the kingdom ... It is certainly consolatory, in a great Commonwealth country, to reflect that there is not a spot, however remote and obscure, along the coast of Sussex and Kent, from Beachy Head to the Isle of Sheppey, on which a vessel might be wrecked, but there are men stationed at all hours of the night ready to give the alarm in an instant and to render able assistance'.

According to the paper, hundreds of people owed their lives to the exertions of the officers and men of the Blockade, all of whom had persistently refused to accept any monetary reward for their services.

In November 1821, during a furious gale, a Danish vessel came ashore between Hastings and Rye, near to Martello Tower number 33, and soon was a complete wreck. Despite heavy surf conditions, three officers from the Blockade managed to launch a six-oared galley from the beach. However, before they had done this, one of the crew of the distressed ship was seen swimming in the angry water and Mr. Drake, Midshipman, immediately attempted to swim to his assistance, carrying a rope, the end of which was anchored by another man on the shore. Amazingly, Drake was able to secure the struggling sailor to the rope and both were pulled to safety. Still with the wreck, however, were the Master, three of the crew, two women and three children. Attempts were made to get a boat out to them, but this capsized, tipping all the would-be rescuers into the boiling sea. Despite further valiant efforts and a second capsize, all the remaining persons were tragically drowned. A little over a month later a French ship, *La Julie* was driven ashore in the same spot and 'the crew were all saved through the prompt and humane exertions of some Officers and men of the Blockade station'.

In March of the following year Mr. Drake was awarded a gold medal by the King of the Netherlands for saving a Dutchman off Winchelsea. Unfortunately, events did not always turn out so happily for the Blockade men, for one was drowned during a rescue of crew from the East Indiaman *Thames* wrecked off Eastbourne in 1822. A Lieutenant and various Midshipmen received rewards for their bravery; the father of the drowned man received 50 guineas to buy a piece of silver plate and a medal worth 5 guineas. Soon after the *Thames* was wrecked a lifeboat, called *The Samaritan,* was delivered to the town from Lowestoft, and placed under the control of the Blockade station there. Two years later the stations at Eastbourne, Seaford and Brighton were supplied with **Captain Manby's Life-Saving Apparatus**. As its name implies, this device was designed to save the lives of shipwrecked mariners, the contraption originally comprising a mortar which fired an iron ball, attached to a chain and a long length of rope. The subsequent addition of a cork cradle on which survivors were supposed to float ashore did little to allay the fears of some, for while the apparatus undoubtedly did save lives, it also caused the loss of one when, in 1826, a young boy was killed by it on Brighton pier, presumably by being struck by the iron ball. The local paper ruefully suggested that it should be renamed the **Death Dealing Apparatus**.

Among the life-saving ideas being thrown around at the time was a particularly bizarre and imaginative suggestion. The lighthouse at the foot of Beachy Head had not yet been built, and one bright spark suggested, tongue in cheek perhaps, that caves should be cut into the chalk at the bottom of the cliffs for the use of shipwrecked sailors, a notice being posted therein printed in eighteen languages. The editor of the newspaper printing the idea was not impressed, sarcastically proposing that the caves be provided with gas lighting, the gas being delivered by Green's airship.

Among the daring rescues undertaken during these years the bravery of one officer deserves special mention. Lieutenant Clark was stationed at Birling Gap and his name appears repeatedly in reports of life-saving by the Blockade. In November 1824, the *Juno* of Jersey grounded at Birling Gap, with a cargo of 1600 bushels of apples aboard. The crew was saved with great difficulty by the prompt assistance rendered by Clark. He and his men were, however, only able to save 1200 bushels of the fruit, subsequently put up for sale at the Newhaven Custom House. Clark was awarded a dress-sword and a gold medal by the vessel's owners. In the same month a Dutch brig, the *Antonia Ulrica* went ashore and Clark was instrumental in preventing the plunder of the cargo, for which he received from the Customs Comptroller plate valued at 5 guineas.

Figure 13: Poster advertising a Sale of Smuggled Goods

In September 1825, the sloop *Ardent*, a 200 tonner from Belfast, ran ashore at Beachy Head with a valuable cargo of linens, corn and provisions. Once again Lieutenant Clark 'eminently distinguished himself under difficult and dangerous circumstances'. He and his men succeeded in refloating the ship and his good manners and cheerfulness were greatly praised by one of the Lloyds agents. 'The many instances of valuable services rendered to ships at Beachy Head and other places by Lieutenant Clark; and at other parts of the strand, by other officers of the Coast Blockade Services, proves their value to the shipping interests of this country'.

Meanwhile, the violence continued. A Blockade sentinel stationed at Haddocks watch house, near Hastings, was attacked with cutlasses, receiving in the process eight head wounds and a severe kicking. Another was taken off the shore one night by smugglers near Bexhill, his murdered body being discovered the following morning. It was not always the lower ranks who were subject to violent assault. Lieutenant Dicken of Rye, who had made the clever discovery of the concealment on the *Diamond* of that port, was attacked in the town only a few days after the seizure of the vessel. The men charged with the assault, Jeremiah Sowden and William Collins, both 28, were probably the owners of the boat. Dicken had been walking with a colleague along Lion Street when the two accused approached from behind, brandishing large wooden clubs. Sowden had said, 'You know, Dicken, you have ruined me, my wife and family, and now I've got you'. Dicken wisely drew his pistol and threatened to shoot, after which the two men were arrested and indicted for attempted murder.

Confirmation and a fuller description of this incident can be found in *The Merry Middies of the Enchantress*, a book of stories written by men who served in the Coast Blockade. According to the author, Dicken had just had dinner with the Collector of Customs at a local inn and was returning to his quarters on the guardship, together with his Portuguese servant, Poncho. According to this account, on being attacked, Dicken 'threw up his arm and the blow fell upon it, fracturing the bone in two places'. Casting a glance round for assistance, the Lieutenant 'saw his cowardly servant, though well-armed and unhurt, crouching under the raised bludgeon of another smuggler called Sowden'.

It appears that the two smugglers were lucky to escape with their lives, as the authorities were not able to prosecute them for the capital felony of 'cutting and maiming'. That offence implied assault with a sharp, rather than blunt, instrument. Nevertheless, they were convicted and sentenced to the maximum possible sentence of two years' hard labour.

There is an interesting postscript to this story. In March of the following year Collins escaped from the House of Correction at Lewes. A year later he was taken by the Blockade after being found on a smuggling vessel, captured whilst running goods in the west. He was conveyed to the *Victory* in Portsmouth Harbour, and thence back to his old quarters in Lewes. We last hear of this man in December 1826. 'Last Tuesday, William Collins, whose punishment for a violent assault of Lieut. H.P. Dicken of the *Ramillies* at Rye*, then expired, was taken into custody by a party of the *Hyperion's* men, for five years servitude on board some one of His Majesty's ships of war ...'

It appears that Sowden, upon obtaining his release, gained admittance into the Coastguard service at Newhaven.

It was not all one-sided; the smugglers, too, suffered terribly at times as a result of their misdeeds. A dreadful event took place a few miles from Hastings when six smugglers, being pursued by a Blockade party, attempted to wade across a deep and steep-sided dyke and were drowned in the process. 'Their bodies were recovered on the following morning, by the assistance of drags; the hand of Gladwish was fixed with a firm grasp round the ankle of one of the Pages, and thus probably both fell victim of a mutual struggle for life. A seventh man named Martin, in attempting to escape, was shot through the heart and instantly expired: and two others were captured without injury'.

* Dicken actually commanded the *Enchantress*, a guard ship stationed on a mud dock two miles below the town of Rye.

Ramillies and *Hyperion*

'The whole of the officers and crew of the *Ramillies* are to be turned over to the *Ganges* and the *Ramillies* is then to proceed to the Downs, where she is to be stationed instead of the *Severn* ... Captain McCulloch is to command the *Ramillies* and the officers and crew of the *Severn* are also to be turned over to her'.

So the *Ramillies* was destined for the Coast Blockade. A 74 gun man-of-war, and the fourth ship to be so named, she had had an interesting history. In 1813, during the war against America, eleven of her crew had been lost after boarding an enemy schooner, blown up by booby-trapped gunpowder hidden below decks. A year later in Chesapeake Bay several attempts were made by the Americans to secure a clockwork mine to her hull by means of a diving-boat. Her Captain eventually dissuaded them from such action by threatening to kill the prisoner he had on board.

Coast Blockade work was somewhat less exciting, and the ship was used principally as a headquarters and punishment vessel for defaulting Blockaders. Her tender, the *Industry*, was regularly employed on trips to Ireland to pick up recruits.

The latter part of 1823 and the early part of 1824 saw the appointment to the *Ramillies* of surgeons and other necessary officers. At the same time arrangements were made for the provision of quarters ashore for the men of the Blockade as they gradually replaced the Coast Guard along the Kent and Sussex coasts. In March 1824 we hear 'The Coast Blockade Service has commenced taking up the stations recently occupied by the Coast Guard. A party of the former with an officer marched into the Martello Tower in Seaford Bay on Thursday last. Another party occupied Bletchington Fort on Friday, and a party commanded by C.W. Poynter, R.N. took possession of Newhaven Battery on Saturday. Their flags are now waving on all the stations between Seaford Head and Porto Bello. The Coast Guard parties retire westward, as the Coast Blockade parties advance, the exchange being effected with the utmost quietness, regularity and good will'.

Figure 14: 'H.M.S. *Ramillies*': Headquarters and punishment vessel for defaulting Blockaders

Arrangements continued apace. By November new watch houses were in hand for Bletchington, Newhaven, Bear's Hide, Saltdean, Rottingdean and Black Rock. A new life boat was commissioned for service at Newhaven.

Captain Mingaye, late of the *Romney*, a 50 gunner, was appointed to command the Blockade Service west of Beachy Head; a depot frigate was to be stationed at Newhaven as his headquarters. An Admiralty Minute of 5 March 1825 was more explicit. 'Write to Captain Mingaye of the *Hyperion* at Newhaven to acquaint him that after he shall have received every information from Captain McCulloch ... he is to consider himself charged with the future superintendence of carrying into execution the said Service making such minor arrangements of this detail as he may deem necessary ... He is to make Newhaven his headquarters but he is to visit all the harbours placed under his management as frequently as conveniently practicable to ensure the active attention to their respective duties, of all those placed under his command'.

Hyperion was a 40 gun frigate (various sources state 36, 40 and 42 guns), which, under the command of one Captain James Lillicrap, had spent the previous two or three years sailing round the Caribbean protecting merchant vessels against the unwelcome attentions of bloodthirsty pirates. She sailed into the calmer waters of Newhaven Harbour at 10 o'clock on a Saturday morning in early March 1825, her permanent mooring being at the spot where the London and Paris Hotel was later built. 'She cuts a noble figure in the water and is distinctly to be seen by the help of a spy-glass, from the yard of St. Annes's church in this town [Lewes]', reported one local journal, while another proclaimed that the ship was towed into Newhaven 'in majestic style by His Majesty's steam vessel *Comet*'. Although the arrival of *Hyperion* was an exciting event for the town's inhabitants, it also put a considerable strain on local accommodation which was eagerly sought by all the ship's officers.

After the arrival of *Hyperion* it seems that McCulloch continued to supervise control of the Kent Blockade, whilst maintaining overall control over the whole force from his command headquarters on the *Ramillies* until his untimely death in October of that year. There is no question that the presence of this new vessel and the accompanying increase in Blockade men in the area must have been a great blow to the local smugglers. Smuggling, however, contrary to the opinion of a local reporter, was not wiped out, neither does it seem to have decreased; it simply became more risky. By 1825 there were no fewer than sixty Blockade stations between Camber in the east and Chichester in the west, including the guard vessels at Rye, Cuckmere, Newhaven and Chichester.

Bribery and Bloody Battles

Bribery and collusion posed a great threat to the efficiency of the Blockade. From the smugglers' point of view it was a better proposition to bribe a Blockade sentinel or two with a relatively small sum of money, thus guaranteeing (they hoped) a clear run, than it was to engage in open and sometimes tragic hostilities. Despite the large number of Blockade stations, the men were vastly outnumbered. Large cargoes necessarily demanded a proportionate body of men to remove them to safety. In view of the possibility of being seriously injured or even killed it is perhaps surprising that **any** of the Blockade men refused bribes in favour of doing their duty.

A writer to the *Brighton Gazette* stated 'bribery has been tried by a gang of smugglers in this town, as a means of corrupting the officers and men of this formidable Blockade system ... Alas! in this too the poor fair traders have lamentably failed. Palm oil, it seems, has not the same mollifying effect on the Blockaders that it used to have on the custom house officers and riding officers of the old regime'.

Francis Hembrey, a liquor merchant and brewer of Hastings, had been fined £100 and sentenced to nine months imprisonment for attempting to bribe a Midshipman from *H.M.S Severn*. Three others involved were similarly treated.

An attempt at bribery occurred at Seaford in 1825, when an Irish Blockade man was offered £20 if he would allow some smugglers to run a number of tubs. The bribe was refused and the matter reported to the commanding Lieutenant, who arrested the men. Twenty pounds was a considerable sum of money and we cannot know why it was refused. Perhaps it was not enough, considering that acceptance would force the sentinel to desert and become a fugitive, or it may simply have been that he was a loyal and honest man. Another incident the following year, when a bribe of only £4 or £5 was offered, suggests that the Blockade men did not always trust the smugglers. 'I have been told by Lieutenant Chappell that the smugglers give the men bad money, farthings instead of sovereigns'.

Punishments for breaches of discipline could be very severe in an age when English naval treatment of offenders was not known for its gentleness. 'The men who compose the great body are driven like slaves to their duty with the cat at their backs, and for the least deviation from the strict line of duty are thrown into the hold, ironed and kept there until the pleasure of their Commander be known'.

On the *Hyperion* floggings took place on Monday mornings, when crowds gathered on the opposite bank to vent their disapproval. One man, William Welch, ordinary seaman, died after having been given forty-eight lashes of the cat for quitting his post and getting drunk. The official cause of death was inflammation of the lungs, and while the inquest admitted that the punishment had been the direct cause of the man's death, they judged that it had been carried out justly and correctly. Because of such punishments some Blockade men deliberately wounded themselves in order to escape from the Service.

When bribery failed to corrupt, violence once more held sway. One Thursday night in May, 1826, the guard boat at Rye was on duty at the mouth of the harbour when she spotted and pursued a smuggling galley. The smugglers beached their boat and began firing on the Blockade men. The sound of gunfire naturally brought out reinforcements from the Camber watch house. At this point, much to the horror of the Blockade, a body of more than two hundred **armed** smugglers rushed from behind the sand dunes, firing as they did so and killing one sentinel, Patrick O'Sullivan, in the process. At the subsequent inquest, with the usual verdict of 'wilful murder against some person or persons unknown', it was revealed that five shots and thirty slugs were removed from the body. The vast sum of £500 was offered as a reward, and Captain Mingaye was moved to request a Bow Street Runner for the town of Rye to assist in the apprehension of the offenders. Notwithstanding this, a spate of bloody affrays followed:

May 18. The Coast Blockade succeeded in seizing a boat with over two hundred tubs but, 'We are sorry to add much mischief has occurred, as the following morning traces of blood were observed near the spot. Two men, it is said, belonging to the boat, are taken prisoners, and two of the Blockade are reported to be much bruised and beaten'. Five smugglers were killed in the fight.

May 30. Smugglers armed with bludgeons seized a sentinel at the 'Old Woman's Tap' near Hastings. The smugglers' boat was later taken by Mr. Blyth, Mate of the *Hyperion* and a £300 reward was offered for the usual information and conviction.

Another incident took place near Bexhill, when Lieutenant Wheeler seized over one hundred tubs, much blood being shed. A special request was made by Mingaye, this time for 50 extra muskets.

February 1827. Lieutenant Digby was attacked with bludgeons at Saltdean, then admonished by the Admiralty for not carrying the required arms. The death sentence was passed on his anonymous assailants.

April 1827. A fatal affray took place near Fairlight involving twenty smugglers and 150 tubs. In addition to using the usual bludgeons, the smugglers seized the Blockade mens' muskets and beat them with the butts. One poor fellow was left for dead with a bayonet in him, with one other dead and the scene covered in blood. A rumour went around that the Blockade was to be superseded by detachments of cavalry, the idea of which greatly amused the *Brighton Gazette*. 'We should like to see the horses galloping over the shingle: they would catch an infinity of smugglers'.

January 1828. The following headline preceded an article in the *Sussex Weekly Advertiser* of the 7th. of that month: **Another Dreadful Conflict,**

between the Coast Blockade, and a Gang of Smugglers, with Loss of Lives. On this occasion the inhabitants of Bexhill were greatly alarmed at 2 o'clock in the morning to be woken by the sound of gunfire. Even they, who must have become accustomed to the frequent scuffles between smugglers and revenue men, can scarcely have believed the ferocity of the battle, for no other word will suffice, which took place near their town on that night. The Blockade had been expecting a run to take place since early the previous evening and had kept a close lookout. They were not disappointed, for at the time stated the boat landed with a cargo of 150 tubs of brandy at the spot where tower number 45 had previously stood. At this time there were only four Blockade men on duty, against a 'company' of nearly seventy, with an additional twenty or so 'batmen'. The Blockade men were marched away by the smugglers and managed to summon reinforcements only after the goods had been got away from the beach. A running battle followed, during which one on each side was killed. During the affray the pistol balls struck the beach with such violence that stones were driven through the windows of the 'Bell Inn'. It was a fine moonlit morning and many of the inhabitants of Bexhill witnessed the outrage from their bedroom windows. The smugglers proceeded directly through Bexhill on the road to Sidley Green, and the officer in command of the Blockade party managed to catch up with them at the Well-Field crossroads at Sidley.

'Here a desperate conflict took place, the batsmen, as before, ranging themselves in trained order, so as to cover the tub-men, who had the care of the well-laden carts. The Blockade party fired upon the smugglers, a close took place, and then the latter began to use their bats. Several of the Blockade were severely bruised by the skilfully directed blows of the batsmen, and the quarter-master (Collins) had his brains literally beaten out. In the first volley fired by the Blockade men the old man, Smithurst, was killed, a bullet entering under the chin and lodging in the chest'.

The smugglers were eventually dispersed, and the whole of the goods barring four tubs were got away. The old man was found the next morning lying dead in the road, with his bat still grasped in his hands, the weapon being almost hacked to pieces by the cutlasses and bayonets of the Blockade men.

Shortly after the inquest was held, a girl came forward and gave information to the authorities about some of the persons involved in this shocking incident. Several men were apprehended and kept in one of the Martello towers for some days. One of the smugglers turned King's evidence and six men were immediately sent for trial at Horsham, more than sixty warrants being issued at the same time.

'Lieutenant Green and his men were out scouring the country, night after night for weeks, in search of the accused persons, and many houses were broken into by main force, in some of which were found the objects of their search, in others they were unsuccessful. The villages round Hastings, for a circuit of 20 miles, were continually in a state of terror and alarm which it is impossible to describe'.

Not surprisingly a number of men disappeared as a result of this exhaustive manhunt; in the parish of Bexhill no less than twenty-five families were 'thrown upon the parochial funds'. One young woman, on seeing her husband dragged from the house by the Blockade, died the following day in a state of madness, while another was delirious for several days following the similar departure of her spouse.

The Final Years

In March of 1829 Captain Mingaye received a memorandum from the Admiralty instructing him to release some of his men for service on the *Melville*, as this vessel's own men were being released to guard the Jersey oyster fisheries. One of the advantages of the Coast Blockade had been that men were available at short notice for a variety of purposes. In 1827, for example, sailors had been taken away for the Navarino campaign. In September, 1829 another request came for men, for the *Melville* again, this time for the Mediterranean service. Two hundred men were shipped off to Portsmouth in *Hyperion*'s tenders, and from thence to the sunnier climes of Malta. In the same month *Ramillies* was taken away for urgent repairs and never again performed Blockade duties, being replaced in the Downs by the *Talavera*. *Ramillies* was eventually broken up in 1850.

When Mingaye had arrived at Newhaven on his frigate in 1825, the whole of the Coast Blockade had employed a total of 2,784 men at an annual cost of £162,740 8s 3d. In addition to the losses of men caused by the country's naval requirements, there was undoubtedly increasing disquiet in official circles about the long-term viability of the force. It had been criticised from the outset on the grounds of cost alone, and the many accounts of violence and death on the coast which appeared in the newspapers cannot have helped the Blockade's cause. The expense in terms of money and human life was unquestionably high, but smuggling had been checked, if not annihilated.

King George IV died in 1830. Only four months after his death a penetrating enquiry was held during which a comprehensive questionnaire was put to Captain Mingaye - designed to obtain answers which would determine the fate of the Blockade. The Captain was asked how many land stations there were, the number of vessels employed, the number of men in the Service, and about the state of smuggling at the extreme ends of the Blockade. The most significant questions related to seizures, of both goods and smugglers, made between 1825 and 1830. The number of tubs seized amounted to 8,404 (equivalent to about 38,000 gallons if a 'tub' is assumed to be the traditional half-anker barrel of spirits), with 40 packages of tea, 255 casks of tobacco and snuff, 106 boats and miscellaneous silks, gloves and other items. 226 smugglers were captured of whom 157 were convicted. It is, of course, impossible to ascertain how much contraband evaded the vigilance of the Blockade and there would have been further seizures made by the Customs officers stationed throughout the county. Did fluctuations in annual seizure figures reflect less smuggling or less prevention? Did the duty payable on the seized goods and the fines imposed (and paid) exceed the cost of administration? There are indeed too many factors outside the scope of this book which need to be examined in order to make a reasoned judgement of the overall effectiveness of the Coast Blockade, and too few statistics produced by the enquiry. What mattered ultimately was whether government **believed** that smuggling was being crushed efficiently, cheaply and quietly enough to satisfy both the Opposition and the British taxpayers.

Apparently it did not. A Treasury note of 31 January 1831 instructed that no further officers or men were to be appointed to the Coast Blockade. A week later an announcement appeared in the *Sussex Weekly Advertiser* to the effect that it was the government's intention to do away with the Blockade, and that the Commanding Officer of the Engineering Department on the coast had received instructions to make an immediate survey of all the towers and other premises occupied by the men and to report upon their state of repair. Enquiry was to be made regarding their market value, condition and letting potential, with a view to possible use by soldiers.

An Admiralty Minute of 23 February left no doubt. 'Captain Mingaye to acquaint the Petty Officers and men of the *Hyperion* that the whole coast will be occupied by the Preventive Service by the second week in April when the Petty Officers will be discharged from the service ... Acquaint Captain Mingaye that Captain Bowles [Coast Guard] has been directed to take immediate steps towards taking possession of the western extremity of the Coast of Selsea and that every facility is to be afforded'.

Following this order men were immediately sent on board the *Kent* and the *Ganges* and Mingaye wrote to the Admiralty in March informing them that the Coast Guard had commenced relieving the Sussex Blockade. A reply followed in a Minute of 31 March. 'Direct Captain Mingaye to send the men under his command to Portsmouth, to be paid off, on their being relieved by the Coast Guard Service'.

The *Brighton Gazette* reported a few days later 'The *Hyperion* will, we understand, very shortly take her departure from Newhaven Harbour. On Saturday last a detachment of the new Coast Guard passed through this place [Lewes] from the eastern part of the county, destined probably for Newhaven or Seaford'.

A subsequent newspaper article stated that the new force had commenced its duties under Customs regulations at Hastings, and that twelve of the 'horse-police' had arrived to perform their interior duty for the prevention of smuggling. 'They are rather well-looking men and are accoutred in a manner calculated for the Service'.

The last Coast Blockade station was relieved on 8 June, 1831. After a turbulent and patchy fourteen years the Blockade, father of the modern Coastguard, sank into the annals of smuggling lore, a curious testament to its enthusiastic, idealistic and largely unsung creator, Captain William McCulloch, R.N.

The End

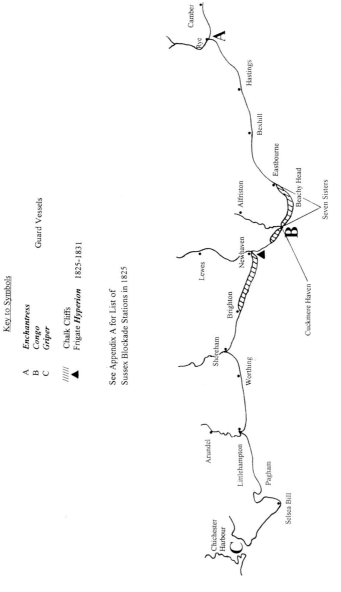

Key to Symbols

A *Enchantress*
B *Congo*   Guard Vessels
C *Griper*

///// Chalk Cliffs
▲   Frigate *Hyperion* 1825-1831

See Appendix A for List of
Sussex Blockade Stations in 1825

Map of the Sussex coastline

Coast Blockade Stations in Sussex, 1825

Camber
Enchantress (Rye Harbour)
Tower 28 *
Greedy Gut
Tower 31
Tower 33
Tower 35
Tower 38
Haddocks
Fairlight
Ecclesbourne
Hastings
Tower 39
Tower 42
Tower 44
Tower 46
Tower 48
Tower 49
Tower 50
Tower 55
Tower 57
Tower 59
Tower 62
Tower 67
Tower 71
Eastbourne
Tower 73 (The 'Wish Tower')
Holywell
Beachy Head >
Birling Gap

Cuckmere Haven
Crowlink
Blatchington
Tower 74
Newhaven (+ *Hyperion*)
Porto Bello
Bearshide
Saltdean
Greenway
Black Rock <
Brighton
Hove
Copperas Gap
Shoreham West
Lancing
Worthing
Kingston
Goring
Littlehampton
Elmer East
Elmer West
Felpham
Bognor
Pagham East
Pagham West
Wall End
Selsey
Thorney
Cockbush
Chichester (Guardship)**

Notes: * Tower 28 etc. - all Martello Towers.
> Beachy Head to Black Rock < - Chalk cliffs.
** I have been unable to ascertain the name of this vessel. In his 'Chronicles of the Customs' (1885), W.D. Chesters mentions a disused brig, the *Griper*, being used by the Coastguard at one time. The Blockade may have used the same vessel during its stay in Chichester.

Sources

Public Records (P.R.O. Kew)

Admiralty Records:
ADM 12 Vols. 180 - 278
ADM 1 Admirals' Letters 753 - 772
ADM 1 Captains' Letters 2182 - 2207
ADM 1 Treasury 4299 - 4301, 4303 - 4306

Newspapers (1816-1831)
The Times
Sussex Weekly Advertiser
Brighton Gazette
Brighton Herald

Periodicals
Gentleman's Magazine 1820 (Vol. XC Part 1)
Sussex County Magazine 1930 p.36